Spinosaurus

Aaron Carr

www.av2books.com

LET'S READ AV² BY WEIGL™
ADDED VALUE • AUDIO VISUAL

Go to **www.av2books.com**, and enter this book's unique code.

BOOK CODE

R904719

AV² by Weigl brings you media enhanced books that support active learning.

AV² provides enriched content that supplements and complements this book. Weigl's AV² books strive to create inspired learning and engage young minds in a total learning experience.

Your AV² Media Enhanced books come alive with...

 Audio
Listen to sections of the book read aloud.

 Video
Watch informative video clips.

 Embedded Weblinks
Gain additional information for research.

 Try This!
Complete activities and hands-on experiments.

 Key Words
Study vocabulary, and complete a matching word activity.

 Quizzes
Test your knowledge.

 Slide Show
View images and captions, and prepare a presentation.

... and much, much more!

Published by AV² by Weigl
350 5th Avenue, 59th Floor
New York, NY 10118

Websites: www.av2books.com   www.weigl.com

Library of Congress Control Number: 2013937450
ISBN 978-1-4896-0596-2 (hardcover)
ISBN 978-1-4896-0597-9 (softcover)
ISBN 978-1-4896-0598-6 (single-user eBook)
ISBN 978-1-4896-0599-3 (multi-user eBook)

Printed in the United States of America in North Mankato, Minnesota
1 2 3 4 5 6 7 8 9 0 17 16 15 14 13

122013
WEP301113

Project Coordinator Aaron Carr
Art Director Terry Paulhus

All illustrations by Jon Hughes, pixel-shack.com.

Spinosaurus

In this book, you will learn

what its name means

what it looked like

where it lived

what it ate

and much more!

Meet the Spinosaurus.
His name means
"spine lizard."

He was one of the largest
dinosaurs that ever lived.
He was bigger than three
elephants together in a line.

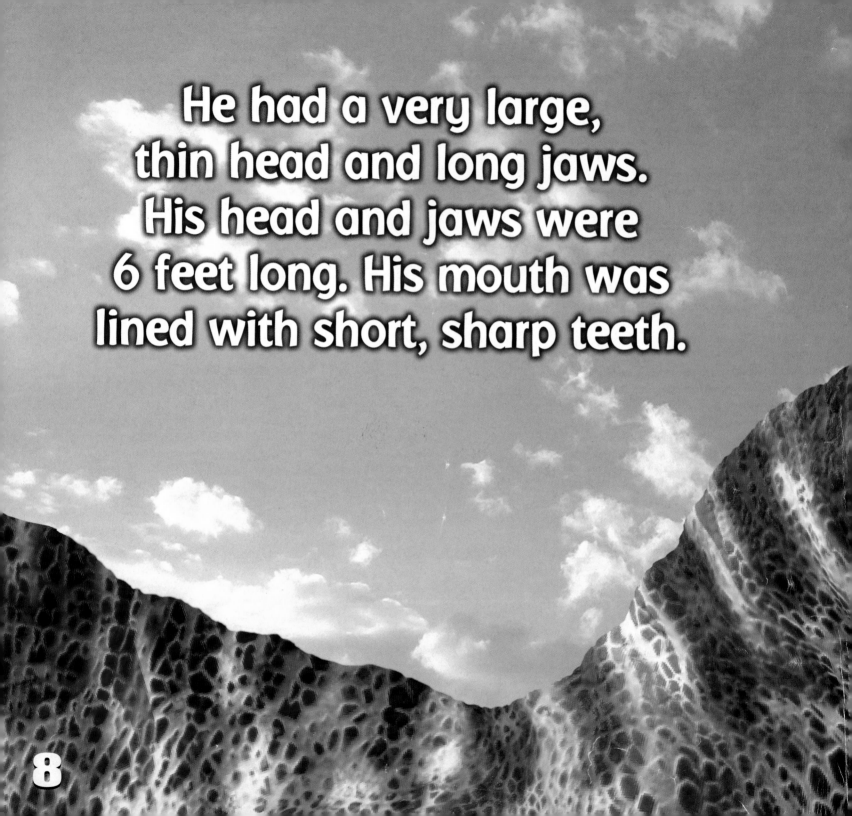

He had a very large,
thin head and long jaws.
His head and jaws were
6 feet long. His mouth was
lined with short, sharp teeth.

He was a meat-eater.
He mostly ate fish and other
animals found near water.

11

He had long bones
sticking out of
his back.

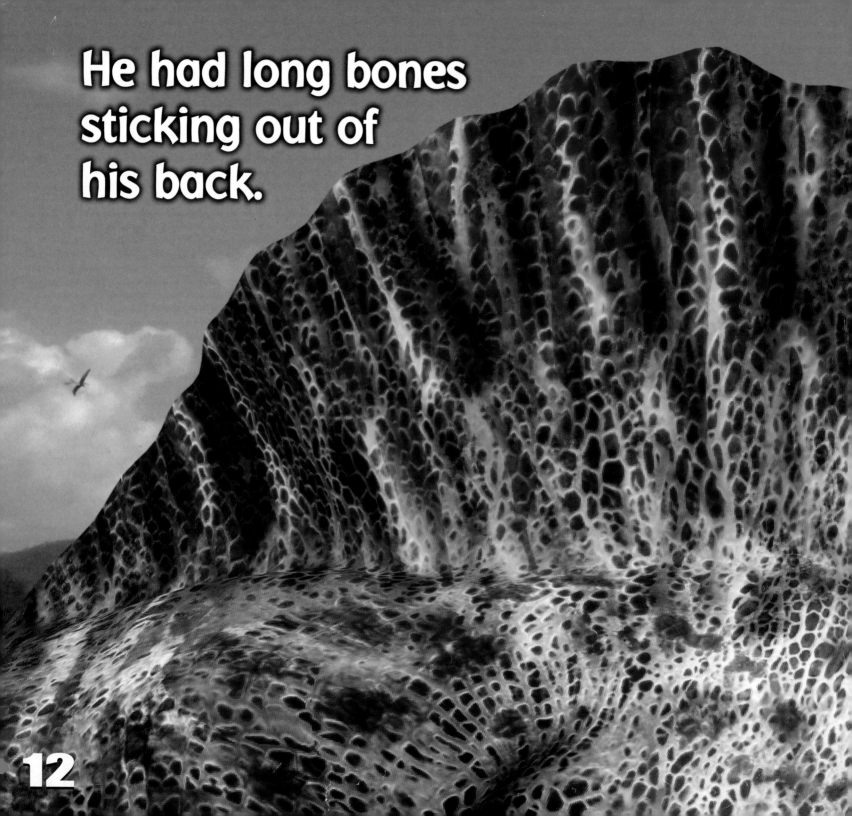

These bones were 5 feet long and covered with skin. This made the bones look like a giant sail.

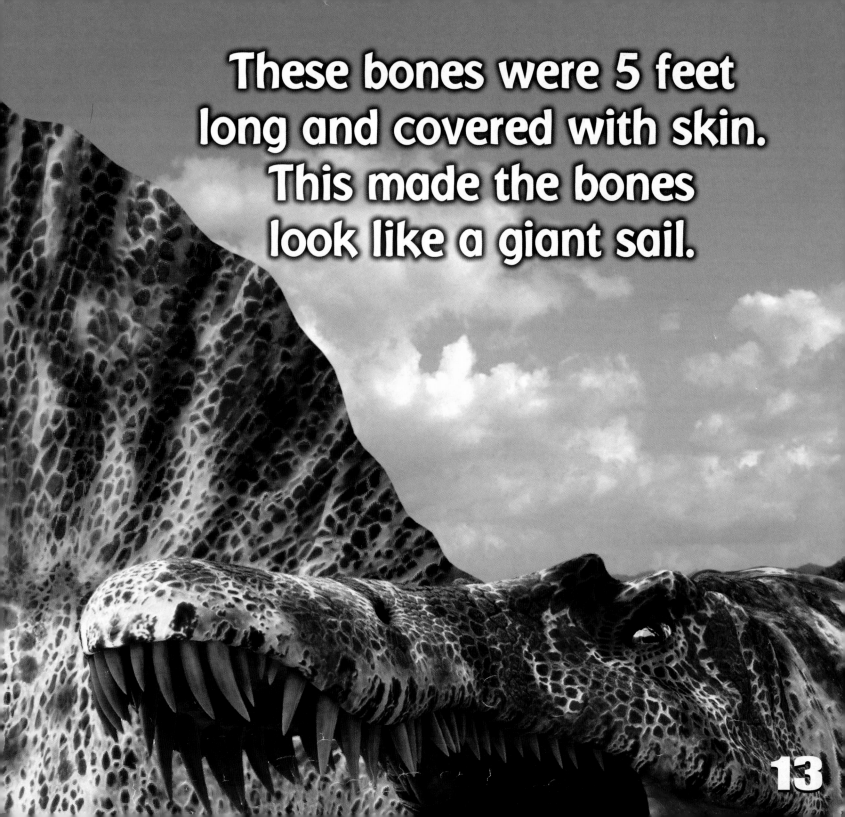

He used his strong back legs
to move quickly.

14

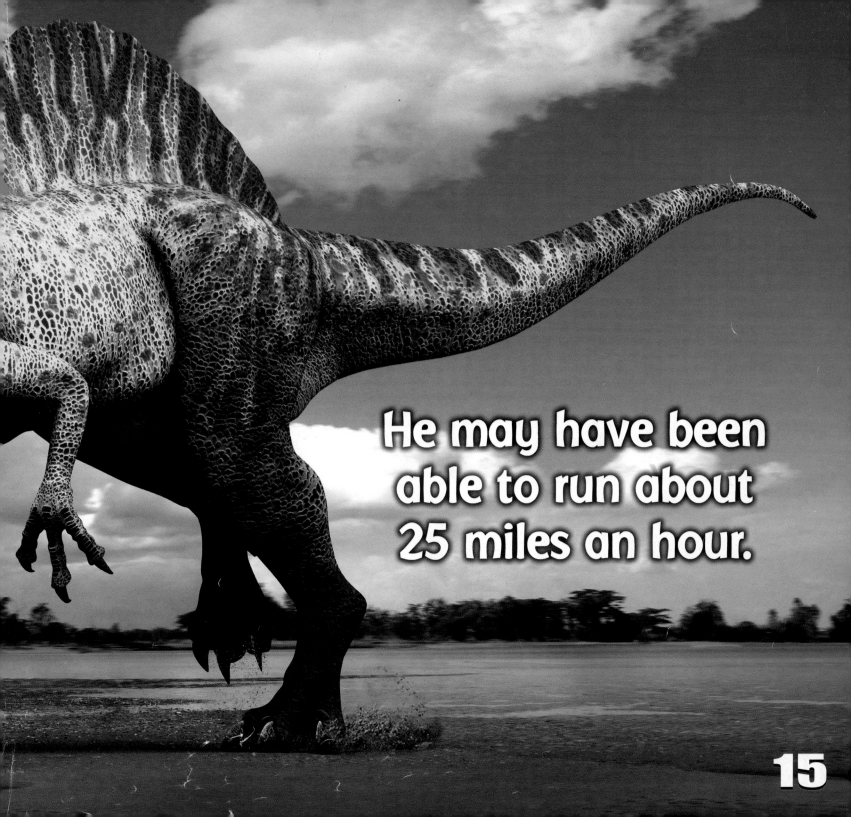

He may have been able to run about 25 miles an hour.

He lived in forest areas
near large bodies of water.

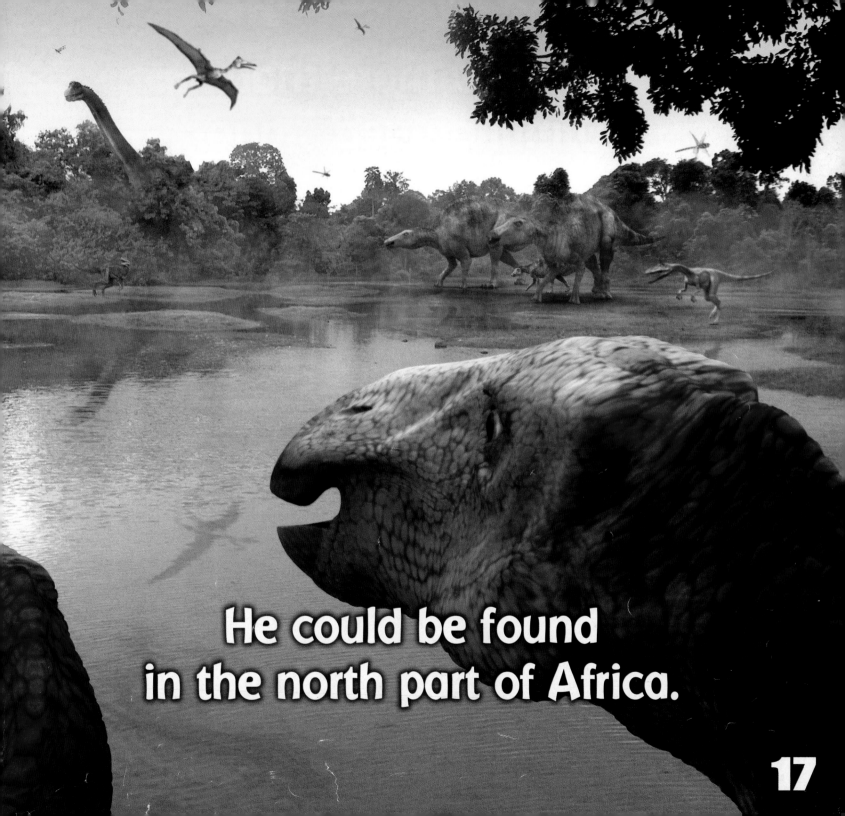

He could be found
in the north part of Africa.

He lived more than
100 million years ago.

People know about him because of fossils.

19

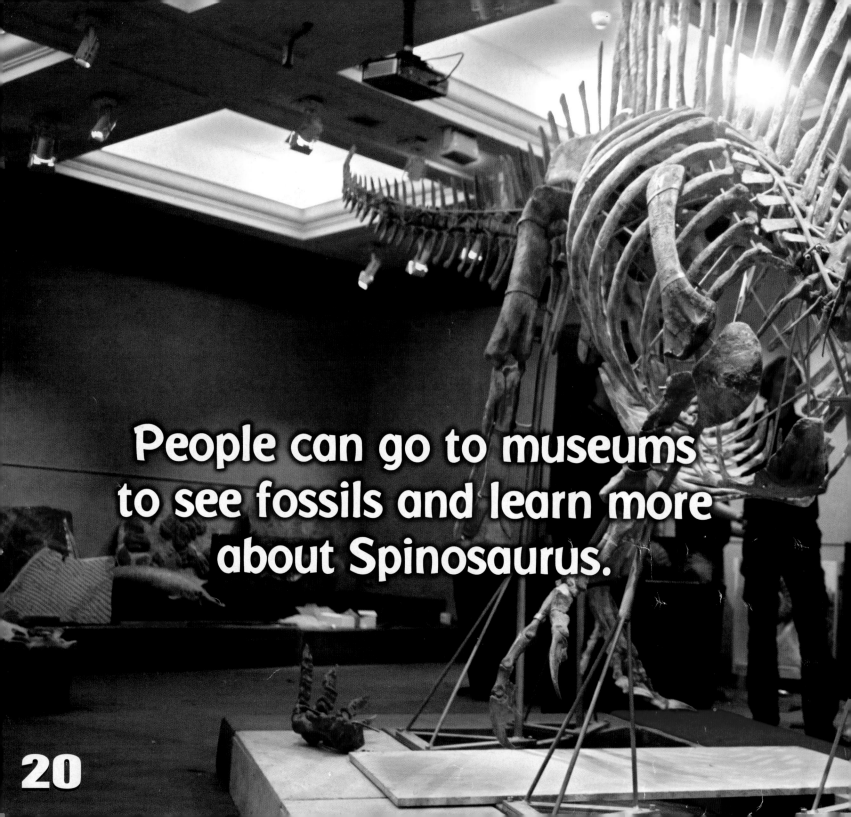

People can go to museums to see fossils and learn more about Spinosaurus.

Spinosaurus Facts

These pages provide detailed information that expands on the interesting facts found in the book. They are intended to be used by adults as a learning support to help young readers round out their knowledge of each amazing dinosaur or pterosaur featured in the *Discovering Dinosaurs* series.

Pages 4–5

Spinosaurus means "spine lizard." Its name comes from the distinct spiny fringe that runs down the Spinosaurus's back. Spinosaurus was possibly the largest predatory dinosaur that ever lived, even surpassing the better-known Tyrannosaurus rex in size and other large carnivores such as Gigantosaurus. Like these other giant carnivores, Spinosaurus was a member of the theropod suborder of dinosaurs.

Pages 6–7

Spinosaurus was one of the largest dinosaurs that ever lived. Both taller and longer than Tyrannosaurus rex, Spinosaurus stood up to 23 feet (7 meters) tall and measured as much as 60 feet (18 m) long. That is taller than a giraffe and almost as long as two school buses lined up end to end. At about 22 tons (24 metric tons), Spinosaurus was also twice as heavy as Tyrannosaurus rex.

Pages 8–9

Spinosaurus had a very large, thin head and long jaws. Its head could be up to 6 feet (1.8 m) long, making it the largest head of any predatory dinosaur. Most of this length was made up of its extremely long crocodile-like jaws. In fact, Spinosaurus had even more in common with the modern crocodile. Spinosaurus had short, straight, pointed teeth instead of the long, curved teeth of other theropods. Like a crocodile, it also had a second palate that allowed it to eat and breathe at the same time.

Pages 10–11

Spinosaurus was a meat-eater. Scientists believe the Spinosaurus's teeth, jaws, and mouth indicate that its main source of food was fish. However, evidence also shows that Spinosaurus ate other dinosaurs as well. It is possible that Spinosaurus may have even preyed on large sauropods. However, some scientist think Spinosaurus may have only eaten food it could find in and around water.

Spinosaurus had a large sail on its back. The sail was made of bones that could be up to 5 feet (1.5 m) long. These bones were part of the Spinosaurus's vertebrae. No one really knows what purpose the Spinosaurus's sail served. It may have helped absorb heat to keep Spinosaurus warm, scare away enemies, or attract mates. However, some scientists believe the sail was filled with fatty tissue that could store water, much like a modern-day camel with its humped back.

Spinosaurus could run very quickly on its two strong legs. Scientists cannot know for sure how fast Spinosaurus was. Some think it may have been able to run about 25 miles (40 kilometers) an hour, while others estimate a lower speed of about 15 miles (24 km) per hour. Like most dinosaurs that walked on two legs, Spinosaurus most likely held its head in front of its legs and its tail stretched behind for balance. However, Spinosaurus may have sometimes used its arms like two additional legs to walk on all fours.

Spinosaurus lived in forests near large bodies of water. It was found throughout northern Africa. At the time Spinosaurus lived, this area was filled with the vast tidal flood plains and mangrove forests. Today, this area is known as the Sahara Desert. Spinosaurus may have lived on both land and sea, much like the crocodiles of today.

Spinosaurus lived more than 100 million years ago. All people know of Spinosaurus comes from fossils, preserved ancient remains of Spinosauruses. Spinosaurus remains have been found in modern-day Egypt, Algeria, Morocco, and Tunisia. The first Spinosaurus fossil was found in 1912, but it was later destroyed in the bombing of Munich, Germany, during World War II. Most of what people know about Spinosaurus actually comes from research notes and drawings made by paleontologist Ernst Stromer in 1915.

People can go to museums to see fossils and learn more about the Spinosaurus. People around the world visit museums each year to see full-sized recreations of Spinosaurus. People cannot see real Spinosaurus fossils because no complete Spinosaurus skeletons have ever been found. Even partial fossils and bone fragments of Spinosaurus are rare. Instead, many museums only have small fossils, such as teeth, on display.

KEY WORDS

Research has shown that as much as 65 percent of all written material published in English is made up of 300 words. These 300 words cannot be taught using pictures or learned by sounding them out. They must be recognized by sight. This book contains 61 common sight words to help young readers improve their reading fluency and comprehension. This book also teaches young readers several important content words, such as proper nouns. These words are paired with pictures to aid in learning and improve understanding.

Page	Sight Words First Appearance	Page	Content Words First Appearance
4	his, means, name, the	4	lizard, spine, Spinosaurus (pronounced: spy-NOH-SAWR-us)
6	a, he, in, line, lived, of, one, than, that, three, together, was	6	dinosaurs, elephants
8	and, feet, had, head, large, lined, long, very, were, with	8	jaws, mouth, teeth
11	animals, found, near, other, water	11	eater, fish, meat
12	back, out	12	bones
13	like, look, made, these, this	13	sail, skin
14	move, to, used	14	legs
15	about, an, been, have, may, miles, run	15	hour
17	be, could, part	16	areas, bodies, forest
18	more, years	17	Africa
19	because, him, know, people	19	fossils
20	can, go, learn, see	20	museums